CORETTA SCOTT KING

and the Story behind the
Coretta Scott King Award

GREAT ACHIEVEMENT
A·W·A·R·D·S

Mitchell Lane
PUBLISHERS

P.O. Box 196
Hockessin, Delaware 19707

GREAT ACHIEVEMENT
A·W·A·R·D·S

Titles in the Series

Alfred Nobel
and the Story of the Nobel Prize

Randolph J. Caldecott
and the Story of the Caldecott Medal

John Newbery
and the Story of the Newbery Medal

Coretta Scott King
and the Story behind the Coretta Scott King Award

Joseph Pulitzer
and the Story behind the Pulitzer Prize

Michael L. Printz
and the Story of the Michael L. Printz Award

Visit us on the web at www.mitchelllane.com
Comments? Email us at mitchelllane@mitchelllane.com

CORETTA SCOTT KING

and the Story behind the Coretta Scott King Award

GREAT ACHIEVEMENT
A·W·A·R·D·S

Printing   3   4   5   6   7   8   9
Library of Congress Cataloging-in-Publication Data
Bankston, John, 1974-
          Coretta Scott King and the story behind the Coretta Scott King Award /John Bankston.
               p. cm. — (Great achievement awards)
Summary: Profiles Coretta Scott King, whose efforts in carrying on her husband's civil rights work led her to establish the Coretta Scott King Award, which celebrates African-American writers and illustrators.
Includes bibliographical references (p.) and index.
          ISBN 1-58415-202-8 (Library Bound)
     1. King, Coretta Scott, 1927—Juvenile literature. 2. African American women civil rights workers—Biography—Juvenile literature. 3. Civil rights workers—United States—Biography—Juvenile literature. 4. African Americans—Biography—Juvenile literature. 5. King, Martin Luther, Jr., 1929-1968—Juvenile literature. 6. African Americans—Civil rights—United States—History—20th century—Juvenile literature. 7. Civil rights movements—United States—History—20th century—Juvenile literature. 8. Coretta Scott King Award—Juvenile literature. [1. King, Coretta Scott, 1927- 2. Civil rights workers. 3. African Americans—Biography. 4. Women—Biography. 5. King, Martin Luther, Jr., 1929-1968. 6. Civil rights movements. 7. Coretta Scott King Award.] I. Title. II. Series.
          E185.97.K47B365 2003
          323'.092--dc21
                                                                                                    2003000346
ISBN 13: 9781584152026

ABOUT THE AUTHOR: Born in Boston, Massachusetts, John Bankston has written over three dozen biographies for young adults profiling scientists like Jonas Salk and Alexander Fleming, celebrities like Mandy Moore and Alicia Keys, master musicians like Franz Peter Schubert, and great achievers like Alfred Nobel. An avid reader and writer, he has worked in Los Angeles, California as a producer, screenwriter and actor. Currently he is in pre-production on *Dancing at the Edge*, a semi-autobiographical film he hopes to film in Portland, Oregon. Last year he completed his first young adult novel, *18 to Look Younger*.

PHOTO CREDITS: Cover: Associated Press; p. 6 Associated Press; p. 8 Bettmann/Corbis; p. 10 Flip Schulke/Corbis; p. Bettmann/Corbis; p. 14 Associated Press; p. 21 Hulton/Archive; p. 28 Associated Press; p. 31 Flip Schulke/Corbis; p. 32 Bettmann/Corbis; p. 34 Bettmann/Corbis; p. 38 Hulton/Archive

PUBLISHER'S NOTE: The following story has been thoroughly researched and to the best of our knowledge represents a true story. Documentation of such research is contained on page 46. This book has not been authorized or endorsed by Coretta Scott King.

          The web sites referenced in this book were all active as of the publication date. Because of the fleeting nature of some internet sites, we cannot guarantee they will be active when you are reading this book.
PLB4,39-45

TABLE OF CONTENTS

CHAPTER 1

Surviving 7

CHAPTER 2

Beginnings 13

CHAPTER 3

Meeting Martin 21

CHAPTER 4

The Struggle 29

CHAPTER 5

Victories 35

Coretta Scott King Award Winners, 1999-2003 41

Coretta Scott King Chronology 43

Events in Coretta Scott King's Lifetime 44

Further Reading 46

Works Consulted 46

Glossary 47

Index 48

For most of her adult life, Coretta Scott King has worked hard for peace and justice. At November 2002's Circle of Hope dinner in San Francisco, she asked for an end to the death penalty in memory of her murdered husband the Reverend Martin Luther King.

CHAPTER 1

SURVIVING

Coretta Scott King sat quietly on the platform in front of Memphis City Hall, waiting for her introduction. After singer Harry Belafonte announced her name, she made her way to the podium. The audience numbered in the thousands: striking garbage workers, civil rights activists, supporters. Her children were just a few feet away. That day as many as fifty thousand people had marched in a demonstration organized by Coretta's husband, the Reverend Martin Luther King Jr.

When the march was planned, Reverend King was supposed to lead them.

Instead, just a few days before, on April 4, 1968, Reverend King was shot to death as he stood alone on a Memphis motel balcony. Coretta had been in Atlanta. When she learned the news, she was devastated but not surprised. Reverend King had predicted his own death. He was hated as much as he was loved.

The day Reverend King was murdered, Senator Robert Kennedy spoke to a troubled nation: "Martin Luther King dedicated his life to love and to justice for his fellow human beings, and he died because of that effort." Kennedy's own brother had been killed by an assassin's bullet less than five years before. He worried some would turn the event into an excuse for further racial division, saying, "black people amongst black, white people amongst white, filled with hatred toward one another."

Just a few days before, Coretta's husband had been murdered. Yet on April 6, 1968 she refused to give up and participated in a garbage worker's strike her husband helped organize. Here she observes a memorial march beside Yolanda and Martin III

The senator, a presidential candidate, would himself be murdered just two months later. On that day, however, he spoke of peace and quoted Greek writer Aeschylus: "In our sleep, pain which cannot forget falls drop by drop upon the heart until, in our own despair, against our will, comes wisdom."

It was the kind of wisdom Coretta prayed for—because all she wanted to do was mourn. She couldn't.

Across the country, in more than five dozen cities, African Americans rioted. In Washington, D.C., they set fires across the capital, and the ashy gray smoke could be seen from the White House. At that moment many Americans wondered if the whole nation would go up in flames. If that happened, Martin Luther King's dreams would die with him. Coretta couldn't let that happen.

The couple had spent over sixteen years together; they had four children. Coretta believed she knew her husband better than anyone. She knew he wouldn't have wanted her to give up.

"I came because whenever it was impossible for my husband to be in a place where he wanted to be, and felt that he needed to be, he would occasionally send me to stand in for him. And so today, I felt that he would have wanted me to be here," she told the crowd in Memphis.

The next day she flew back to Georgia and buried her husband.

It was uncomfortably hot as mourners made their way to the brick Ebenezer Baptist Church in Atlanta. Inside, his funeral was attended by senators and congressmen, everyone from the Vice President to President John F. Kennedy's widow, Jackie.

Martin's father peered out over the crowd, his voice filled with passionate rage as he said, "It was hate in this land that took my son away from me."

Despite the despair of her husband's death, Coretta refused to give in to hatred.

Even before she met Martin, Coretta was a strong woman, toughened from growing up in the segregated South. After they married, Coretta was not the stereotypical old-fashioned housewife. On her own she gave speeches and helped Reverend King organize bus boycotts,

At her husband's funeral, Coretta heard messages of rage and messages of hope. Courageously when it was her chance to speak she spoke of love, justice, peace and "brotherhood where all men can truly be brothers."

sit-ins, and voting registration drives. As the wife of Reverend King, she'd survived bombing attempts and death threats. Now she was alone.

"How many men must die before we can really have a free and true and peaceful society?" she had asked the crowd in Memphis. "How long will it take? If we can catch the spirit and true meaning of this experience, I believe that this nation can be transformed into a society of love, of justice, peace and brotherhood where all men can truly be brothers."

Over the next four decades, Coretta would do all she could to turn her husband's ideals into reality. In 1969, the American Library Association honored Martin Luther King's memory and Coretta Scott King's continuing work for peace and brotherhood by establishing the Coretta Scott King Awards, which celebrate African-American writers and illustrators. As recognized by the award, Coretta's many good works place her among the world's great achievers.

From the early days of their marriage, Coretta often spoke whenever Dr. King was unavailable. After his death, she continued to honor his memory by giving speeches and championing various social causes.

BEGINNINGS

S lavery ended more than sixty years before Coretta was born. With a stroke of Abraham Lincoln's pen and the loss of over 500,000 lives in the Civil War, African Americans were given their freedom.

In the South they were given little else.

After the Civil War, Yankee troops maintained order in the southern states during a period called Reconstruction. Shortly after the troops pulled out, the rights of African Americans were slowly eroded. The highest court in the land believed the so-called Jim Crow laws were permissible under the U.S. Constitution. In the 1896 *Plessy v. Ferguson* Supreme Court decision, "separate but equal facilities" were declared legal. From then on the color of a person's skin determined which section of a theater or bus they sat in. Bathrooms and water fountains had signs for "white" and "colored." It was "the very worst period of the repression of African Americans since the days of slavery," Coretta explained in her autobiography, *My Life with Martin Luther King*. The laws made African Americans feel anything but equal. However, Coretta's father, Obadiah "Obie" Scott and his wife, Bernice, made sure their children grew up knowing they were as special as any white child. They proved it by hard work and determination, valuing education, and demonstrating that even the biggest obstacles didn't have to get in the way of a person's dreams.

From movie theaters to water fountains, a person's skin color determined their place in Jim Crow society. Here Mississippi police chief George H. Guy proudly poses beside a Greyhound bus station segregation sign.

When Coretta Scott was born on April 27, 1927, in Heiberger, Alabama, her father was probably the most successful black man in Marion County. He and his family, which included Coretta's older sister Edythe and her younger brother Obie, lived in a two-room house on his father's 300 acres. Coretta was barely able to walk before she began laboring on the property, picking corn and other vegetables, feeding the hogs and chickens.

Meanwhile her father ran a successful business selling pine logs from the land to sawmills. On weekends, he cut hair. A trained barber, he often had men lined up around the house waiting for a haircut and some conversation.

However, despite the Scotts' best efforts to pull together, when Coretta was less than three years old the country entered into a time known as the Great Depression. Following the stock market crash of 1929, unemployment rose to 25 percent, and poverty and homelessness increased enormously. In the South, rural farms were hard hit by droughts.

Life was very difficult. One of the things Obie was known for was his truck, which he made payments on. No other African American man in the area drove his own truck. In the 1930s, making those payments became impossible, so Obie gave the truck's title to a white business-man. That meant the white businessman would continue to make payments for Obie, but Obie would have to work off the debt. The businessman owned the sawmill where Obie sold his pine logs, and for a long time it looked like Obie would always be in debt.

He wasn't alone. Many farms were being sold for very low prices as farmers were unable to make mortgage payments. Despite the challenges, Coretta grew up sheltered somewhat from the racism of the South. The Scotts lived on a hill, with acres of land between them and their neighbors in a predominantly black county. Eventually she became aware of racism, learning hard lessons at the corner drugstore.

In the 1930s, the corner drugstore was the place to go for sodas and ice cream. For many white adults, the corner drugstore is a sweet memory. For Coretta it was a place where she couldn't go through the front door because of the color of her skin, and no matter what flavor ice cream she asked for, the clerk would just dish out whatever he had too much of.

In her autobiography Coretta remembered eventually asking her mother why things were the way they were. "You are just as good as anyone else," her mother told her. "You get an education and try to be somebody. Then you won't have to be kicked around by anybody and you won't have to depend on anyone for your livelihood—not even a man."

Bernice worked hard to install those values in her children, although she herself had barely made it to the fourth grade. Despite their lack of formal education, both of Coretta's parents made sure there were books in the house, and Coretta's mother often read her bedtime stories.

Valuing education in the 1930s South wasn't easy for African Americans, especially since the state government didn't seem to care if they got an education or not. Coretta began attending elementary school when she was six. It was five miles from her house, but, unlike the white kids, Coretta didn't ride on a school bus. She walked. White children received their education in a beautiful brick building divided into classrooms. African-American children were educated in a run-down one-room schoolhouse. White children got their textbooks for free. Coretta had to pay for hers, working for a neighboring farmer picking cotton in the blistering heat for less than ten dollars a summer. The white school year was two months longer, as if the state didn't think black students needed to know as much and were of better use in the fields.

Still, the Scott family persevered. Obie finally paid off his truck and rented a six-room house. And at twelve years old, Coretta was able to go to the private Lincoln High School with her older sister (Obie Jr. would attend as well). The $4.50-a-year tuition for each of them wasn't easy to come up with, but the Scotts believed the sacrifices were worth it.

Lincoln High School was founded shortly after the Civil War by northern missionaries who believed African Americans were just as entitled to a quality education as white students. Although it always had an all-black student body, by the time Coretta began attending, some of the teachers were black and others were white. The white teachers, who were from up North, endured a fair amount of abuse from local whites who didn't appreciate "Yankees" coming down and teaching in a "colored" school.

Because she lived so far away, Coretta boarded in Marion with a family that took in a number of Lincoln students. She only saw her parents on weekends. In Coretta's junior year, the Scotts and a few other families convinced Marion County authorities to provide money for transportation—an enormous victory. Not only was Coretta able to move back home, but her mother began driving one of the buses, which her father built from one of his trucks.

Coretta found more than a quality education at Lincoln. She found a love for music. Coretta learned to read music, became a decent trumpet player, and even used an instrument called a flutaphone. She also took basic piano. However, the instrument Coretta worked on the most was her own—she took singing lessons, becoming an accomplished member of the school's choir.

But even as Coretta's life was transformed by school, tragedy touched her family. It was Thanksgiving in 1942 and Coretta was still in Marion with her sister when they got a phone call from Heiberger. Someone had set their house on fire. The family home burned to the ground.

The Scotts never found out who was responsible, and the police refused to investigate. Just a few months later, the sawmill her father built was also torched. Again, the local police refused to get involved. Despite the setbacks, Coretta claims in her autobiography that her father never became disheartened or bitter, reminding her, "There are some good white folks."

In 1945, Coretta graduated from Lincoln as class valedictorian—she had the highest grades in her class. She also had her pick of colleges. Once again she decided to follow Edythe's lead.

Ohio's Antioch College was a small liberal arts school with an outstanding music program that had just begun offering scholarships to a few talented African-American students. Ever since Edythe's admission, she'd sent letters home to Coretta, detailing what a great school it was and promising her sister that she'd be very happy there.

Edythe's letters didn't tell Coretta everything.

Coretta knew Antioch was the right school for her. The only concern she had was that, although the school drew students from across the country, most of the students there were white. There were a number of black colleges that would have welcomed her, like Spelman and Morehouse, but they were in the South.

At eighteen years old Coretta knew one thing: She didn't want to stay in the South, even if it meant going to a school where she was one of the few African Americans.

When she arrived at Antioch in the fall of 1945, she discovered a school every bit as open, friendly, and challenging as her sister described it. It was so challenging that Lincoln's class valedictorian struggled academically despite working very hard. "Like most southern students," Coretta recalled in her autobiography, "I had such an inadequate educational background that even Lincoln had not prepared me properly." By her second semester, Lincoln's star student had to enroll in a remedial reading program.

Although the step took a great deal of courage and humility, afterward she began to catch up to her peers. Unfortunately there was a race wall between Coretta and her classmates. In all of her glowing descriptions of Antioch, Edythe did not tell Coretta about the way she was treated by the school's white majority. Sure, they weren't as openly hostile in their prejudices as southern whites, but they were prejudiced nevertheless. Coretta found that many of her conversations in cafeterias and dorm rooms revolved around race, as if she were the spokesperson for the entire African-American community.

Social interactions were just as challenging—despite being an attractive young woman, Edythe rarely dated at Antioch. For her part, Coretta resisted being paired with the only African-American man in her class, instead dating a white man from New York.

Coretta's harshest experience with northern prejudice was one she could have duplicated south of the Mason-Dixon Line (a line separating Pennsylvania and Maryland, considered the boundary between the northern and southern states). As an education major she was expected to student teach for two years—handling teaching duties at a local school under the supervision of a professional teacher. Her first year she taught at the private high school run by Antioch.

The problems arrived in her second year. Coretta was assigned to teach at a local public school. Although the student body was integrated—there were both black and white students—the teachers were all white. The principal of the school refused to allow an African American to teach there. Even more hurtful, when Coretta went to her dean at Antioch, he told her there was nothing he could do. He refused to protest on her behalf.

Coretta was given a choice: She could teach in a segregated school with black teachers or she could do a second year at the private high school. She stayed with the private high school. She hadn't traveled all the way from Alabama to teach in a segregated school.

Coretta graduated in 1951. She knew exactly what she wanted to do for a living. She wanted to be a professional singer. The best schools for her were either Juilliard in New York City or the New England Conservatory of Music in Boston, Massachusetts. What she didn't realize was that the choice she was about to make wouldn't just affect her career. It would affect her whole life.

When Coretta Scott met the young Martin Luther King Jr. she was surprised by how short he seemed. Yet as they got to know each other he seemed to increase in stature. His powerful voice and courage convinced most of his listeners that he was a far larger man than he really was.

CHAPTER 3

MEETING MARTIN

The world Martin Luther King Jr. knew was every bit as segregated as Coretta Scott's. However, while Coretta's parents knew little but struggle, by the time of Martin's birth his father was already very successful, living in an upper-middle-class neighborhood near Auburn Avenue, home to some of the most successful African Americans in Atlanta, Georgia.

Martin was born on January 15, 1929, in his parents' bedroom. His mother was fairly permissive, but his father, whom everyone called Daddy King, was a hard-driving minister who worked to instill ambition in his oldest son. In Marshall Frady's biography *Martin Luther King Jr.,* a neighbor recalled Daddy King exclaiming that "he would make something of him even if he had to beat him to death."

Whether or not the regular "whippings" had anything to do with it, Martin often *was* the best. Although he struggled with spelling and grammar, his vocabulary and overall understanding of school subjects was far ahead of his classmates'. By age fifteen he'd skipped enough grades to go on to college. He enrolled at Morehouse College, a prestigious university that educated the children of many of Atlanta's African-American elite.

Although Martin's opportunities were available to very few African Americans in the 1940s, he wasn't immune to the era's prejudices. He often experienced the bigotry of a "separate but equal" society, but he also witnessed his father's steely courage. A policeman once pulled over the family car. When he made the mistake of calling the senior King "boy," according to the Frady biography, Daddy King looked hard at the white officer and, pointing to young Martin, said, "That's a boy. I'm a man."

Perhaps Daddy King's response was on Martin's mind as he stood during a ninety-mile return trip from an academic outing. After presenting a well-received paper entitled "The Negro and the Constitution," the teen was forced to stand during the bus ride home because white passengers had taken all the available seats. He did nothing that day. But later, he would make a difference for thousands of African-American passengers who had had to abandon their seats for whites.

Although Martin had a great deal of respect for his father, as he studied at Morehouse they clashed repeatedly over Daddy King's plans for his oldest son. The minister viewed the Ebenezer Baptist Church as something of a family business, like a carpet store or a health club. He fully expected Martin to take over the pulpit.

Martin had other ideas. He was filled with questions about religion, and he thought there were better ways to make a difference in society. For a time he considered a career in law or medicine. Yet in his academic career, few works inspired him as much as Henry David Thoreau's *Civil Disobedience,* an essay that explained how to fight against unjust rules.

And then, quite suddenly, Martin decided to do what his father wanted him to do. He became a minister. From his own accounts and those of friends, there was no "divine inspiration" or "calling." He just decided that becoming a minister might be a good way to change the lives of African Americans after all. In Frady's biography, Martin's sermons are remembered as "a respectable force for ideas, even social protest." After his graduation from Morehouse, he became an assistant pastor at Ebenezer. From the first time he took the pulpit and preached, he was transformed. His voice was stronger, clearer. He seemed more of a man, less of boy.

He also discovered an excellent use for his well-developed vocabulary.

In the fall he left for Crozer Theological Seminary in Chester, Pennsylvania. About 25 percent of the student population was African American, an almost unknown level of integration in the 1950s. In spite of the mixture, he felt compelled to set an example, and frequently argued with fellow black students who broke the rules by hiding beer in their room or otherwise conducted themselves in a way he felt reflected badly on other African Americans.

His attitude didn't win him any popularity contests. Often alone, he spent his time reading, studying everything from the philosophy of Nietzsche and Hobbes to the communist dictates of Marx. He began studying the nonviolent protests of Mahatma Gandhi. The methods Gandhi used to gain independence for India would have a profound effect on Martin's life.

It wasn't until his second and third years that Martin began to open up and become more relaxed. He started drinking beer with other students, and smoking—a lifelong habit he'd work hard to conceal from photographers and most supporters. He also started dating regularly. Martin's intelligence, smooth tongue, and fashion sense made him popular with women, but in his third year Martin took some serious risks with his romantic life.

Less than a year from graduation, he began dating the daughter of a German immigrant who worked in the school cafeteria. Before she began going out with Martin, she'd been dating a professor. But it was less her romantic history than her color that made things difficult. His new girlfriend was white. This was a time when interracial dating wasn't just discouraged, in some southern states it was still illegal.

The romance bloomed, in spite of society. Martin fell in love. He knew his parents would have a hard, if not impossible, time accepting her. He knew it would make preaching to an African-American congregation unlikely. Yet he still pursued the relationship. He told his friends he wanted to marry her. They were flabbergasted; many of them tried to talk him out of it.

Finally, he realized society wasn't where he'd like it to be. It was ironic: the changes he wanted to effect would make interracial dating less controversial, yet it would be impossible for him to bring about those changes if he married a white woman. After a tremendous amount of soul-searching, his choices drove him into a deep depression.

Eventually he broke up with the girl. According to his closest friends, Martin never got over it. What he didn't know at the time was that he was just a few months from meeting the woman who would help him forget his heartache.

Coretta decided against New York City and Juilliard. She'd already spent a summer in New York and found it to be too crowded, too dangerous. She believed Boston would be more livable. After graduation from Antioch she focused on the New England Conservatory and what she believed would be the training for her professional career.

The summer after her graduation, she also decided to stop relying on her parents. She applied to the Jessie Smith Noyes Foundation for a grant. Unfortunately, Coretta quickly learned that all the available grants had been awarded; she'd be placed on a waiting list. If someone turned down a grant, she'd get the money.

Coretta returned home for a brief stay in Alabama. "Although my father could have afforded to send me to the conservatory, I decided not to ask him," she recalled in her autobiography. "I had been dependent long enough. I would go to Boston whether or not I had a scholarship."

Before she left for Boston, her father asked her what she'd do if she didn't get the money. Coretta confidently told him she'd work full-time and go to school part-time. The bravado was an act: Coretta was very worried about her future. Despite her fears, she got on the train for Boston with nothing more than fifteen dollars and hope.

The gamble paid off. While waiting to change trains in New York, she called home. A letter from the foundation had just arrived in Alabama—Coretta was getting $650. The money would cover her tuition and fees, but she still needed to figure out a way to take care of herself.

In Boston, Coretta boarded with a woman on Beacon Hill who offered a number of conservatory students a room and breakfast for a dollar a day. It was a reasonable price for the city, but it was more than Coretta could afford. The fifteen dollars in her purse was going fast. Her first night in Boston, she feasted on peanut butter and graham crackers. There would be a lot of peanut butter that first year.

Money was a constant struggle. To pay for her room, she scrubbed floors on her hands and knees, washed linen, worked as a cashier and part-time at the Urban League. Her dedication paid off. Her classes were fulfilling, and she developed a professional-quality singing voice. By her second year, she earned more scholarships, including a $100 award from Alabama. The state provided money to African-American students who studied out of state because they couldn't get the classes they wanted in Alabama's black colleges. The money was one way Alabama kept its schools segregated.

While Coretta struggled, across town at Boston University, Martin Luther King Jr. was studying for his Ph.D. in theology. He'd graduated from Crozer at the top of his class, and academically his life at BU was going well. Socially, it was another story. After breaking up with his girlfriend at Crozer, he learned that his parents expected him to marry a girl he barely knew. As far as Martin was concerned, he'd followed his father's wishes with the ministry; he wasn't about to let him choose his wife.

Despite his conviction, he couldn't connect with the young women he met in Boston. In desperation he asked a friend of his, Mary Powell, if she knew any women he'd be interested in. She did.

Mary knew Coretta from the conservatory and thought the two would do well together. She gave a glowing description of Coretta, but when she told Coretta what Martin did, she recalled in her autobiography, "The moment Mary told me the young man was a minister, I lost interest, for I began to think of the stereotypes of the ministers I had known." The ministers she'd seen back home were judgmental and not at all fun—hardly boyfriend material.

Reluctantly she let Mary give Martin her number. When he called, he quickly erased her prejudice—he was smooth and charming and, best of all, funny. She agreed to a lunch date the next day.

On a rainy January afternoon, Martin picked up Coretta in his green Chevy—having made the ten-minute trip in seven. When he exited his car, Coretta was disappointed: He seemed so short and ordinary-looking. Yet as the date progressed she was touched by his sincerity and impressed by his intelligence. With every minute he seemed to grow taller. It was an experience that millions would someday share.

The oddest part of the date came at the end. As the two sat in his car, Martin quietly told Coretta, "The four things that I look for in a wife are character, intelligence, personality and beauty," as she recalled in her autobiography. He quickly added, "And you have them all."

Coretta was taken aback. In the 1950s, couples in their late teens and early twenties courted, formal dating which often led to marriage. It was impossible to go out with someone and *not* picture a possible wedding. Still, bringing up marriage on a first date was very odd, even for 1952.

That night, alone in her room, Coretta recalled thinking, "I didn't want anything to stop me, to stop my career." The last thing she needed was to marry a preacher when she wanted to be a singer.

Coretta's worries didn't keep her from going out with Martin again. He was interesting and persistent, and with every date her feelings for him grew deeper. Almost without realizing it, she fell in love. Despite his first-date proclamation, Martin had his own worries. He'd assumed, given her Antioch education, that Coretta would not be able to under-stand the less-educated churchgoers. He didn't realize how poor she'd been as a child, or that her parents had never finished high school.

While Martin worried about whether or not Coretta would fit in as a preacher's wife, Coretta turned to religion for her answer. She prayed and prayed, hoping to make the right decision. In the end her sister convinced her. Yes, marrying Martin might mean giving up her singing career, but it didn't mean giving up on a career. Coretta would never be "just" a housewife. It was obvious from listening to Martin's ambitions that a life of adventure awaited whoever married him.

By the time Coretta decided to marry Martin, the only obstacle was his parents. They believed Martin was breaking a commitment—a commitment to a girl he barely knew. It took a few icy visits before Coretta stood up for herself. She told them that she had something to offer too.

The couple married during the summer before their last year at school. They were wed on June 18, 1953, in the backyard of the Scotts' newly purchased home. Daddy King performed the ceremony. In it Coretta promised to love and honor. She had the words *to obey* removed from her vows. After all, she knew she and Martin would be partners. She just didn't know exactly what that would mean.

Rosa Parks never intended to start a movement. She was tired and didn't feel like giving up her bus seat. Her choice, and her arrest led to the Birmingham Bus Boycott. Here she's being fingerprinted two months later for violating Alabama's segregation laws.

CHAPTER 4

THE STRUGGLE

Rosa Parks was tired. It was December 1, 1955, and after a long day of work as a tailor's assistant, she was ready to go home. She did some shopping and waited for her bus. When she boarded, it wasn't crowded, so she paid her fare and made her way to the center. She sat down in the first row in the black section.

As an African American in Montgomery, Alabama, Rosa wasn't allowed to sit anywhere near the front of the bus. That section was reserved for whites.

As the bus continued toward Rosa's home, it filled up. Most of the passengers who got on were white. Rosa Parks had ridden the bus hundreds of times, so she must have known what was coming.

At the next stop, the driver shouted that he needed some of the passengers in the black section to free up a few seats. They were needed for the white bus riders. Reluctantly a few African Americans stood and moved farther back. Rosa didn't. She was too tired, and her feet hurt. Although she didn't realize it then, by refusing to move, refusing to give up her seat and thus allowing herself to be arrested, Rosa's act of civil disobedience would launch a movement.

This movement would eventually grant African Americans civil rights they'd been denied for over seventy years.

Rosa wasn't the only African American in Montgomery who was tired. Many members of the city's African-American community were tired: tired of separate and *un*equal facilities, tired of harassment by whites, tired of laws and a justice system that didn't treat them fairly. In late 1955, African Americans in Montgomery decided to do something about it.

When E. W. Dixon, the former president of the National Association for the Advancement of Colored People (NAACP), called Ralph Abernathy, the minister of the First Baptist Church, he asked him who he thought was the best person to organize the city's leadership. Abernathy knew exactly whom to call—the young dynamic minister who'd just taken over Dexter Avenue Baptist Church: Martin Luther King Jr.

A lot had happened since Coretta and Martin married in 1953. She'd graduated from the New England Conservatory of Music and was giving lessons part-time to help pay the bills. Martin had continued to pursue his doctorate, and for a while Coretta imagined they'd stay up North while she figured out a way to pursue her singing career.

Everything changed when he was offered the ministry at Dexter Avenue Baptist Church in Montgomery. When he told Coretta about the job, she was nervous. "Having come from a town in Alabama only about eighty miles from Montgomery, I knew the situation there only too well," Coretta explained in her autobiography. "I knew from my own life, that in this city, living in its memories as the first capital of the Confederacy, the stifling hood of segregation at its worst would soon drop over us. I also felt that Montgomery would offer me little opportunity or challenge in pursuing my musical interests."

Despite her concerns, Coretta knew marriage was a partnership, and she decided Martin had the better opportunity. They moved to Montgomery. Until June 1955, when Martin received his doctorate, he regularly commuted to Boston to work on his thesis. Even more challenging, on November 17, Coretta gave birth to their first child— Yolanda Denise. So when Martin's friend Ralph Abernathy asked for his help, the couple's plate was already quite full.

Martin was a member of the NAACP and had already served on a committee that protested bus company policies. Unfortunately, he'd made little progress, learning that far from being a united front, the city's African-American community was deeply divided along class and educational lines.

While Coretta and her husband are idolized for their work in the civil rights movement, in the beginning they were like many young married couples struggling to raise a happy family. Here Coretta enjoys some piano time with Yolanda, Bernice and Marty

Coretta recalled in her book that Dixon told Martin, "We have taken this type of thing too long. I feel the time has come to boycott the buses. It's the only way to make the white folks see that we will not take this sort of thing any longer."

Martin agreed to run the meeting of local leaders at the Dexter Avenue Church. Later he told Coretta that while he was pleased with the turnout—over forty showed up, including prominent lawyers, doctors, and a bunch of ministers—the meeting quickly descended into chaos. No one seemed to be able to agree on anything except for the need to boycott. So he made that the focus.

And twenty-six-year-old Martin found himself leading men twice his age. He was nervous, but he also learned what a great team he and Coretta made. They set Monday, December 5, as the first day of the boycott. There wasn't much time. All day Saturday Martin organized leaders in the community and convinced black cab company owners to

Out in front and standing tall beside her husband, Coretta Scott King joins Martin in a civil rights demonstration on the state capitol in Montgomery, Alabama. This is the end of a five-day March.

give bulk discounts and set up carpools. At home Coretta worked the phones, coordinating rides and meetings.

On Sunday Martin, like most other African-American ministers in Montgomery, urged his congregation to support the boycott and stay off the buses. Despite the efforts, Coretta knew there was no way they'd get the message out to all 50,000 African Americans in the city. They didn't have to: The white-owned newspaper did the job for them. In a scathing editorial, the paper opposed the boycott while managing to promote it to every black reader in the city.

Sunday night there was little sleep in the King household.

Monday morning Coretta rose at 5:30 A.M. and waited in the living room to watch the six-o'clock bus pass by their house. "Right on time the bus came, headlights blaring through the December darkness," Coretta recalled in her autobiography. "I shouted, 'Martin! Martin! Come quickly!' He ran in and stood beside me, his face lit with excitement. There was not one person on that usually crowded bus!"

From that chilly day in December on, Montgomery's African Americans carpooled, cabbed, biked, or walked—anything to avoid paying the fare on a segregated bus. Martin himself took an additional leadership position, gaining the presidency of the newly formed Montgomery Improvement Association (MIA). Across the country newscasts carried stories about the young African-American preacher from Montgomery.

Martin's success enraged racist whites. Coretta fielded most of the harassing phone calls. Her husband was usually away at meetings or giving speeches, as he was on January 10, 1956, when she and a friend heard a loud thump against the porch. The two ran to the back bedroom, where two-month-old Yolanda was sleeping. It was a bomb! The explosion ripped apart the porch and blasted glass into the living room. Coretta remembered how unhelpful the police had been with her father—perhaps they had been involved. She didn't call them, but the cops still arrived, rushing into the crowd of angry African Americans who'd surrounded the Kings' damaged home. Martin came home to a near riot. There was shouting and cursing while he struggled to make sure his family was okay.

They were fine, but outside all hell was breaking loose.

Coretta described in her book how Martin stepped outside onto the broken porch and appealed for calm. It was "his first deep test of his Christian principles and his theories of non-violence." It would have been easy to respond to the violent attack by inciting further violence. Instead Martin told the crowd, "I want you to go home and put down your weapons. . . . We must meet violence with non-violence." As they relaxed, he continued, "Remember if I am stopped, this movement will not stop, because God is with this movement."

It was the first time Coretta heard Martin speak of his own death. It wouldn't be the last. Coretta realized she'd have to live her life knowing the man she loved might someday be murdered for the cause he believed in.

Being the leader of a civil rights movement meant constant risk of arrest. Here Dr. King is led away by officers O.M. Strickland and J.V. Johnson for the crime of loitering near a courtroom. He later claimed to have been beaten and choked by the officers.

VICTORIES

It took over a year and a Supreme Court ruling before the buses of Montgomery, Alabama, were desegregated. On December 21, 1956, Martin celebrated by riding on the first integrated bus alongside Rosa Parks, Ralph Abernathy, and E. W. Dixon.

Martin's fame grew as a result of the victory. He made the cover of *Time* magazine. Reporters from all over the world began calling the King house. However, in Alabama, Martin paid the price for the exposure, as he was arrested for everything from speeding to failure to file income tax returns. He won most of the cases against him, but it was still difficult and took time away from his cause.

Coretta's price was different. As her husband's influence grew, he was gone more and more often. She was left at home to deal with their growing family (they would have a total of four children) and doing much of the paperwork and phone calls for the MIA and the newly formed Southern Leadership Council (SLC). As president of SLC, Martin traveled frequently between Montgomery and the organization's Atlanta headquarters. He also oversaw voter registration drives and sit-ins; he gave speeches and lectures. By the early 1960s Martin was gone over 200 days a year.

The separations took their toll on the marriage, as did a weakness of Martin's. "Each of us is something of a schizophrenic personality," Martin told a group of college students, according to biographer Frady. "We're split up and divided against ourselves. There is something of a civil war going on within all our lives. Within the best of us there is some evil, and within the worst of us there is some good." Martin was a human being, not a god, thrust into the center of a civil rights battle that would consume the rest of his life. As the stress grew, so did his weakness for women. According to Frady, Coretta and Martin fought over his infidelities, although she later said, "All that other business just doesn't have a place in the very high level relationship we enjoyed." She also admitted Martin was "guilt ridden" because he didn't believe he deserved the lofty position he'd been put in.

In many ways theirs was a modern marriage, as Coretta did her own share of traveling, organizing church leaders, celebrating Women's Day in Denver as a keynote speaker, and traveling to Geneva, Switzerland, to ask for a halt to atomic weapons testing. In some cases Coretta faced prejudice because she was female, but she persevered, as Martin had in the face of racial prejudice. She also used her vocal training, singing in Freedom Concerts and helping to raise money for various causes alongside professional singers like Harry Belafonte.

For the Kings, a near tragedy reminded them yet again of how uncertain life could be. During a book signing in New York City, Martin was stabbed in the chest with a letter opener by a crazed fan. It wasn't a racial attack—the woman was African American—but the incident brought the King family closer.

As the 1960s dawned, protests ripped across the South. On campuses and in cafeterias African Americans rebelled against "separate but equal" laws. In many of these actions, Martin or Coretta was leading the way—sometimes seeming to be in several places at once. Martin faced sheriffs and mayors, even governors, who fought the nonviolent protesters with fire hoses, dogs, and wooden batons. Using the types of passive resistance techniques Martin had learned about on trips to India and in books on Gandhi, the protesters laid down in streets and on sidewalks. To achieve desegregation, Martin himself was jailed dozens of times. Once it took a phone call from President Kennedy to give Coretta a chance to speak with her imprisoned husband.

Yet even as he was jailed, even as tragedies in the form of bombings and murders took place in the South, battles were being won. In June

1963, President Kennedy announced his support for civil rights legislation that would make racial segregation illegal in any public facility.

Two months later, on a steamy August day in Washington, D.C., Martin spoke from the steps of the Lincoln Memorial to 250,000 supporters. The words of that speech are now world famous. He told the assembled, "I have a dream that my four little children one day will live in a nation where they will not be judged by the color of their skin but by the content of their character."

The work to achieve that dream continued, despite a horrible setback. On November 22 that same year, President Kennedy was killed in Dallas, Texas. However, the civil rights legislation he'd promoted did not die with him. His successor, President Lyndon B. Johnson, signed the bill into law on July 2, 1964, with Martin Luther King Jr. by his side. That year, Martin received the Nobel Peace Prize, a tremendous honor.

Over the next four years the Kings continued to promote civil rights and nonviolence. They fought for voting rights. They lived for a time in public housing in Chicago to illustrate the plight of poor African Americans who lived in cities. They also began to help African Americans who were trying to assemble unions, believing that fair working conditions were a part of civil rights. At every turn, Martin's life was in danger.

Martin's murder could have destroyed the movement. But as he wished, the movement survived his death. Coretta's work honoring his name and his legacy continues.

Meanwhile, the family has also dealt with the question of who killed Martin. James Earl Ray confessed to the killing but later recanted. Coretta Scott King believes Ray acted as part of a larger conspiracy. In December 1999 a Tennessee jury found that the assassination was indeed the result of a conspiracy, but by the time of their decision the man who'd been imprisoned for the crime had already died in jail.

In 1969 she published her autobiography, *My Life with Martin Luther King Jr.* Her connection to the publishing industry deepened that same year when librarians Glyndon Flynt Greer, Mabel McKissack,

Besides championing civil rights and social justice, Coretta Scott King has also championed literacy. The award given in her name honors the best of African-American writers for young adults. Here she poses with the book she wrote, My Life with Martin Luther King, Jr.

Roger McDonough, and publisher John Carroll designed an award to honor the late Dr. King's work and Coretta's continued efforts to promote civil rights, education, and world brotherhood. Overseen by the American Library Association (ALA), a panel of judges awards the prize each year to an African-American writer "whose distinguished books promote an understanding and appreciation of the American

Dream," according to the ALA's Web site. The award for illustrator was added in 1979. Winners receive a framed citation, an honorarium, and a set of *Encyclopaedia Britannica* or *World Book Encyclopedia.*

In the thirty-plus years since the award's inception, it has joined the Newbery and the Caldecott Awards as a major honor for writers and illustrators who work in literature for young adults. In *Black Issues Book Review,* author Virginia Hamilton said, "The thirty-year history of the Coretta Scott King Award needs to be woven deeply into American literature."

Perhaps it already has been. Most members of the literary community saw the need for a separate prize for African Americans over three decades ago, but recently this separation has been questioned. After all, Hamilton won both the Newbery and the CSK. In an article for *The Horn Book,* Marc Aronson argued, "By insisting on testing the racial identity of its winners, the CSK shifts its focus from literature to biography. Who you are, which box or boxes you check on the census form, comes first."

Aronson points out that other awards don't ignore African-American writers, but the CSK ignores all writers who aren't African American (unless they are collaborators in a story).

Coretta felt that the United States had a long way to go before African Americans were truly equal, and she worked diligently to prod the country along. After her husband's death, she raised funds to build the Martin Luther King Jr. Center for Nonviolent Social Change, which she founded in Atlanta, Georgia. The center opened in 1969. Now known as simply the King Center, it covers three city blocks and includes a library and the largest archives of the civil rights movement. She was president and chief executive officer of the center until 1995, when she handed the reins to her son, Dexter Scott King.

While overseeing work at the center, King succeeded in achieving another major goal—to get her husband's birthday honored as a national holiday. Meanwhile she continued working on her overall mission: doing what she could to make her husband's dream of fairness and equality come true. In that vein she devoted time and energy to organizations such as the National Council of Negro Women, whose mission statement includes "helping women of African descent to improve the quality of life for themselves, their families and communities," the Black Leadership Forum, the National Black Coalition for Voter Participation, and the Black Leadership Roundtable. In 1985 she and three of her children were arrested for demonstrating against apartheid. Later, she visited South Africa, meeting with businessmen and anti-apartheid leaders. She spoke out against the Haitian military regime that oppressed Haitian citizens, and in 1993 she urged the United Nations to "reimpose an embargo against the nation."

She received honorary degrees from forty universities.

In speeches to college students, Coretta frequently quoted Horace Mann, the founding president of Antioch: "Be ashamed to die until you have won some victory for humanity." When Coretta Scott King died on January 30, 2006, she had won much victory for humanity.

THE CORETTA SCOTT KING AWARD

Coretta Scott King Award Winners, 2000–2005

(For a complete listing of all Coretta Scott King Award Winners, 1970–Present, see http://www.ala.org/srrt/csking/winners.html.)

Author Award Winners

2000   *Bud, Not Buddy* by Christopher Paul Curtis (Delacorte)

2001   *Miracle's Boys* by Jacqueline Woodson (G.P. Putnam's Sons)

2002   *The Land* by Mildred Taylor (Phyllis Fogelman Books/ Penguin Putnam)

2003   *Bronx Masquerade* by Nikki Grimes (Dial Books for Young Readers)

2004   *The First Part Last* by Angela Johnson (Simon & Schuster)

2005   *Remember: The Journey to School Integration* by Toni Morrison (Houghton Mifflin)

Author Honor Books

2000   *Francie* by Karen English (Farrar, Straus and Giroux)

Black Hands, White Sails: The Story of African-American Whalers by Patricia C. and Frederick L. McKissack (Scholastic Press)

Monster by Walter Dean Myers (HarperCollins)

2001   *Let It Shine! Stories of Black Women Freedom Fighters* by Andrea Davis Pinkney, illustrated by Stephen Alcorn (Gulliver Books, Harcourt)

2002   *Money-Hungry* by Sharon G. Flake (Jump at the Sun/ Hyperion)

Carver: A Life in Poems by Marilyn Nelson (Front Street)

2003   *The Red Rose Box* by Brenda Woods (G.P.Putnam's Sons)

Talkin' About Bessie: the Story of Aviator Elizabeth Coleman by Nikki Grimes (Orchard Books/Scholastic)

2004   *Days of Jubilee: The End of Slavery in the United States* by Patricia and Frederick McKissack (Scholastic)

Locomotion by Jacqueline Woodson (Grosset & Dunlap)

The Battle of Jericho by Sharon Draper (Atheneum)

2005   *The Legend of Buddy Bush* by Sheila P. Moses (Margaret K. McElderry)

Who Am I Without Him? by Sharon Flake (Jump at the Sun)

Fortune's Bones by Marilyn Nelson (Front Street)

Illustrator Award Winners

2000 *In the Time of the Drums,* illustrated by Brian Pinkney; text by Kim L. Siegelson (Jump at the Sun/Hyperion Books for Children)

2001 *Uptown* by Bryan Collier (Henry Holt)

2002 *Goin' Someplace Special,* illustrated by Jerry Pinkney; text by Patricia McKissack (Anne Schwartz Book/ Atheneum)

2003 *Talkin' About Bessie: The Story of Aviator Elizabeth Coleman*, illustrated by E.B. Lewis (Orchard Books/ Scholastic)

2004 *Beautiful Blackbird* by Ashley Bryan (Atheneum)

2005 *Ellington Was Not a Street* illustrated by Kadir Nelson (Simon & Schuster)

Illustrator Honor Books

2000 *My Rows and Piles of Coins,* illustrated by E. B. Lewis; text by Tololwa M. Mollel (Clarion Books)

Black Cat by Christopher Myers (Scholastic)

2001 *Freedom River* by Bryan Collier (Jump at the Sun/ Hyperion)

Only Passing Through: The Story of Sojourner Truth illustrated by R. Gregory Christie; text by Anne Rockwell (Random House)

Virgie Goes to School with Us Boys illustrated by E.B. Lewis; text by Elizabeth Fitzgerald Howard (Simon & Schuster)

2002 *Martin's Big Words,* illustrated by Bryan Collier; text by Doreen Rappoport (Jump at the Sun/Hyperion)

2003 *Rap A Tap Tap: Here's Bojangles-Think of That*, illustrated by Leo and Diane Dillion (Blue Sky Press/ Scholastic, Inc.)

Visiting Langston, illustrated by Bryan Collier (Henry Holt & Co.)

2004 *Almost to Freedom* illustrated by Colin Bootman (Carolrhoda)

Thunder Rose illustrated by Kadir Nelson (Silver Whistle)

2005 *God Bless the Child* illustrated by Jerry Pinkney (Amistad)

The People Could Fly illustrated by Leo and Diane Dillon (Alfred A. Knopf)

CHRONOLOGY

1927	Born in Heiberger, Alabama, on April 27
1937	Begins picking cotton to earn money to pay for textbooks
1938	Graduates from Crossroads School; enters Lincoln High School
1945	Graduates from Lincoln High School as valedictorian; enters Antioch College, majoring in music and education
1951	Graduates from Antioch; enrolls at New England Conservatory of Music
1952	Introduced by a friend to Martin Luther King Jr.
1953	Marries Martin Luther King Jr. on June 18 in Marion, Alabama
1954	Graduates from New England Conservatory of Music with degree in voice and violin; relocates to Montgomery, Alabama, with Martin
1955	On November 17, Yolanda "Yoki" Denise King is born; African Americans begin Montgomery bus boycott on December 5; Martin made president of Montgomery Improvement Association
1956	King home is firebombed
1957	Coretta attends a meeting of African-American ministers in Atlanta; son Martin Luther King III is born on October 23
1958	Gives a speech at Denver's New Hope Baptist Church celebrating Women's Day
1960	The Kings move to Atlanta
1961	Gives birth to Dexter Scott on January 30
1962	Joins forty-nine other women as delegation to Geneva, Switzerland, demanding an atomic weapons ban
1963	On March 28, Bernice Albertine King is born
1966	King family moves to public housing in Chicago, Illinois, to publicize the difficulties of urban poverty
1968	On April 4 Martin Luther King Jr. is assassinated on a motel balcony in Memphis, Tennessee
1969	Founds Martin Luther King Jr. Center for Nonviolent Social Change in Atlanta; the American Library Association establishes

continued on next page

the Coretta Scott King Award; publishes her autobiography, *My Life with Martin Luther King Jr.*

1983   Brings together more than 800 human rights organizations to form the Coalition of Conscience, sponsors of the 20th Anniversary March on Washington

1985   With three of her children, is arrested at an anti-apartheid demonstration

1986   Prevails in her campaign to establish a national holiday honoring Dr. King

1987   Helps lead the national Mobilization Against Fear and Intimidation in Forsyth County, Georgia

1988   Reconvenes the Coalition of Conscience for the 25th anniversary of the March on Washington

1995   Turns over leadership of the King Center to her son, Dexter Scott King

2003   Continues to speak out against injustice, especially racial injustice, doing what she can to make her husband's dream of fairness and equality come true.

2006   Dies, January 30

EVENTS IN CORETTA SCOTT KING'S LIFETIME

1919   Across the country over two dozen race riots claim hundreds of lives, including seventy African Americans lynched across the South.

1929   The stock market crash marks the beginning of a period known as the Great Depression, when many lose their jobs.

1941   In June, President Franklin Delano Roosevelt creates the Fair Employment Commission to assure nondiscrimination practices in federal hiring; the December sneak attack by the Japanese on Pearl Harbor drives the United States into World War II.

1947   Jackie Robinson joins the Brooklyn Dodgers, becoming the first African American to play in major league baseball.

1948   U.S. armed forces integrate the troops.

continued on next page

1954	In their *Brown v. Board of Education of Topeka* decision, the Supreme Court rules that separate schools are unequal and therefore unconstitutional, reversing the *Plessy v. Ferguson* decision of 1896.
1957	When the Little Rock High School in Little Rock, Arkansas, is desegregated, Governor Faubus puts National Guard troops in place to prevent African-American children from going to the school. When over 1,000 federal troops are brought in to escort the students, the governor closes schools for a year.
1962	When African-American student James H. Meredith enrolls at the previously all-white University of Mississippi, over 5,000 federal troops are needed to protect him.
1963	The head of the Mississippi NAACP, Medgar Evers, is murdered; President John F. Kennedy is assassinated in Dallas.
1968	Presidential candidate and John F. Kennedy's brother Robert Kennedy is assassinated in Los Angeles; Martin Luther King Jr. is assassinated in Memphis.
1969	Man first walks on the moon.
1978	The Supreme Court rules that racial quotas are illegal in college admissions, but affirmative action programs that give advantage to minorities are deemed constitutional.
1992	In Los Angeles, over fifty people are killed during rioting sparked by the acquittal of police officers who beat black motorist Rodney King.
1999	A jury in Memphis, Tennessee, concluded in *Coretta Scott King, Martin Luther King, III, Bernice King, Dexter Scott King and Yolanda King v. Loyd Jowers and Other Unknown Conspirators* that Loyd Jowers and government agencies including the City of Memphis, the State of Tennessee, and the federal government were party to a conspiracy to assassinate Martin Luther King Jr.
2003	President George W. Bush denounces direct preferences for racial minorities in college admissions. He has his administration file a brief with the Supreme Court arguing that the affirmative action admissions policies at the University of Michigan amount to a quota system and should be declared unconstitutional.
2005	King children consider selling the King Center

FURTHER READING

F O R   Y O U N G   A D U L T S :

Patrick, Diane. *Coretta Scott King.* New York: Franklin Watts, 1991.

Press, Petra. *Coretta Scott King: An Unauthorized Biography.* Westport, CT: Heinemann, 2000.

Rediger, Pat. *Great African Americans in Civil Rights.* New York: Crabtree Publishing, 1996.

Rhodes, Lisa Renee. *Coretta Scott King.* Philadelphia: Chelsea House, 1998.

Schraff, Anne. *Coretta Scott King: Striving for Civil Rights.* Berkeley Heights, NJ: Enslow, 1997.

Siegel, Beatrice. *The Year They Walked.* New York: Four Winds Press, 1992.

Taitz, Henry, Sondra Taitz and Emily Taitz. *Coretta Scott King: Keeper of the Dream.* Berkeley Heights, NJ: Enslow, 1992.

O N   T H E   I N T E R N E T :

Edwards, Roanne. "King, Coretta Scott."
http://www.africana.com/Articles/tt_038.htm

The King Center.
http://www.thekingcenter.org/csk/bio.html

W O R K S   C O N S U L T E D :

Frady, Marshall. M*artin Luther King, Jr.* New York: Viking, 2002.

King, Coretta. *My Life with Martin Luther King Jr.* New York: Henry Holt and Company, 1969, 1993.

Medearis, Angela Shelf. *Dare to Dream: Coretta Scott King and the Civil Rights Movement.* New York: Lodestar Books, 1994.

American Library Association. "Coretta Scott King Award."
http://www.ala.org/srrt/csking/index.html

"Coretta Scott King"
http://www.galegroup.com/free_resources/whm/bio/king_c_s.htm

The King Center
http://www.thekingcenter.org/tkc/index.asp

Pappas, Heather. "Coretta Scott King." The Nuclear Age Peace Foundation.
http://www.wagingpeace.org/articles/peaceheroes/coretta_king.htm

GLOSSARY

affirmative action	(ah-FER-mah-tiv AK-shun) an active effort to improve the opportunities of minorities and women in the job market and in receiving an education.
apartheid	(ah-PAR-tight) the policy of apartness, or segregation, especially when referring to the discrimination against non-European groups in South Africa.
assassination	(ah-SA-sen-AY-shun) the murder of an important person for political reasons.
boycott	(BOY-cot) a protest in which a group decides not to purchase a certain product or support a certain business.
civil disobedience	(SIH-vel dis-oh-BEE-dee-ense) refusing to obey laws one regards as unjust, usually to make a political statement.
embargo	(im-BAR-go) an order of a government that bars trade with another government or country.
Jim Crow	slang term for discrimination against African-American people that was allowed by law or custom.
integration	(in-tah-GRAY-shun) to allow people of all races to blend and be equal in society; the opposite of *segregation.*
nonviolence	(non-VIE-oh-lence) using only peaceful means to achieve political goals.
passive resistance	(PASS-iv re-SIS-tense) a form of protest in which the protester does not fight or struggle but allows himself to be arrested.
prejudice	(PREH-jeh-diss) anger or bias toward members of a certain group without regard to their civil rights; a negative opinion formed without just cause or enough knowledge.
quota	(KWOE-tuh) a number that represents a fair portion of minorities in the total population rather than the fair portion of minorities among qualified applicants.
segregation	(seh-grih-GAY-shun) the policy of separating ethnic groups or races in such areas as employment, housing, or education.

INDEX

Abernathy, Ralph   30, 35

Aeschylus   9

Aronsot, Marc   39

Belafonte, Harry   7, 37

Carroll, John   38

Coretta Scott King Award   37-39

Dixon, E.W.   30, 35

Gandhi, Mahatma   23

Greer, Glyndon Flynt   37

Hamilton, Virginia   39

Jim Crow Laws   13

Johnson, Pres. Lyndon B.   37

Kennedy, Jackie   9

Kennedy, John F.   9

Kennedy, Sen. Robert   7

King, Coretta Scott

    at Antioch   17-19

    at Lincoln High   16-17

    at N.E. Conservatory   24

    birth of   14

    early years   15-16

    marriage to Martin   26

    Montgomery Bus Boycott   31-33, 35

    public speaking   36, 39-40

King, "Daddy"   9, 21-22, 27

King, Rev. Martin Luther

    birth of   7

    death of   7, 37

    education of   21 – 24, 25, 30

    marriage to Coretta   26

    Montgomery Bus Boycott   31-33, 35

    New York City attack   36

Nobel Peace Prize   37

McDonough, Roger   37

McKissack, Mable   37

NAACP   30

Parks, Rosa   29, 35

Ray, James Earl   37

Scott, Bernice   13, 15

Scott, Edythe   14, 16, 17, 26

Scott, Obadiah "Obie"   13, 14, 15, 16

Scott, Obie   14, 16

Thoreau, Henry David   22